Life Around
Saul Ju

Gateway to the World

ISBN No. 978-0-9561743-2-1
Published by the Cotswold Canals Trust
in partnership with the Junction Heritage Project, September 2011
2 Bell House, Wallbridge Lock, Stroud, Glos., GL5 3JS
Content includes contributions of local people to be found on
www.junctionheritage.org.uk
Editors for the Junction Heritage Project: Iris Capps and Lois Francis
Edit and layout: David Jowett 01453 755535
Print liaison: Sharon Kemmett at The Design Co-operative 01453 751778
Printed by StroudPrint 01453 764251
Front cover picture taken around a hundred years ago
Picture above courtesy Stroud District Council taken 2006
Back Cover photo taken August 2011

www.cotswoldcanals.com

About This Book
by Iris Capps, Chairman, Junction Heritage Project

The Junction Heritage Project was born out of an idea suggested by British Waterways and the Cotswold Canals Trust that a local group should collect memories and facts about the waterways that meet at Saul Junction and the people who live in the surrounding villages and towns. Storage and management presented early problems and thus a website seemed to be the most practical way forward. Hence www.junctionheritage.org.uk was born and thrives to this day.

This book contains but a small selection from the website together with other articles. Our thanks go to all of our contributors and readers. All of the material in this book has been donated by the various contributors to the Junction Heritage Project and copyright remains with the original authors or photographers. They are; Michael Handford. Lois Francis, Liz Young, Wing Commander John W Vick, Richard Merrett, Pattie Butt, Daphne Hinman, E A Blackman, Antony Jones, Bob Merrett, Tony Ashby, Mike Mills, Ian Parkin, Brian Ward Ellison and David Jowett. Thanks too to Phil Trotter at the R W Davis & Son boatyard.

The following have been unfailing in their support and advice. Many thanks to Joan Tucker, Hugh Conway-Jones and Paul Barnett.

Large vessels are rare visitors these days

The view from Saul Junction looking north-east (above) and south-west (below) with Sandfield Wharf buildings and Cadbury's factory just visible either side of the tree on the top left

Around Saul Junction
by Lois Francis (with thanks to Hugh Conway-Jones)

Over time, the Stroudwater Canal has had an enormous influence on the type of businesses, housing and transport of the area. It was built in 1779 whereas the Gloucester to Sharpness Canal was opened early in the 1800s creating the waterway crossroads. Both canals have been substantially researched and written about by Michael Handford, Joan Tucker and Hugh Conway-Jones and the reader who wants to delve deeper would be advised to seek out their books.

We start a tour of the features that can be seen around Saul Junction nearly a quarter mile from the junction itself.

A - Walk Bridge was originally a steeply arched bridge carrying a private road that belonged to the Whitminster Estate over the Stroudwater. Over time, residents of Saul used the road to get to and from Bristol Road. In 1885 the then owner of the estate, Mr H.H. Wilton paid for it to be replaced by a swing bridge which subsequently had to be modified to allow the ship canal company's steam dredger to pass. The swing bridge was replaced by Gloucestershire Highways when the canal company agreed to an Act of abandonment in 1954. The new bridge was fixed and so ended navigation beyond.

B - The Marina was built during 2007 and opened in 2008. The site gradually filled to become a popular mooring facility with a capacity of 284 boats.

C - The Junction of two canals. Saul Junction is the only place in the country where there is a level intersection of two independent canals. The Stroudwater Canal, built along the valley of the River Frome, was opened in 1779 to allow barges to carry coal from the Forest of Dean up to the industrial communities of the Stroud Valleys. The deeper Gloucester and Sharpness ship canal was constructed to avoid parts of the River Severn that were difficult to navigate and was constructed between 1818 and 1827.

In order to accommodate the River Frome, and various landowners who wanted to keep their rights over water supply, the course of the Stroudwater was tinkered with and a substantial change made when the Gloucester and Sharpness Canal was built. The initial Junction of the two canals was about 40 yards north-east of the present position, behind the Junction House with the water then being at the existing level of the Stroudwater, and the first barges were able to pass between the two canals in February 1820. However, when the ship canal was filled to its full level, the Stroudwater had to be raised about four feet to suit.

D - The Present Lock and Junction were built on a new alignment, as commissioned during the summer of 1826, after the old line was closed off. Today, the canal bends as it approaches the ship canal whereas it initially ran straight, behind Junction House.

There are no plans to restore the Stroudwater Canal from here to the Severn although some sections remain in water.

E - Junction House adjoining the Junction was built for the official whose duties included recording traffic passing from one canal to the other and collecting tolls where appropriate, supervising the lock and stop gates when necessary and opening the footbridge which carried the towpath of the Stroudwater Canal over the ship canal. Some of the activities required to run a modern canal are still undertaken from the office here.

F - The Junction Boatyard was for many years shared by private boatbuilders and the ship canal company's craftsmen. The boatbuilders built and repaired small sailing vessels, and the craftsmen constructed and maintained bridges, lockgates and maintenance craft. Apart from providing the usual boatyard services, RW Davis & Son Ltd is now well known for its sturdy narrowboats which are highly sought after.

G - The Dry Dock was built in 1869 across one corner of the Junction with gates to allow vessels to move easily between the two canals as it had already become apparent that the Company's dredger was too large to turn the sharp corner.

Today, the dry dock is often used to maintain the hulls of smaller leisure boats and larger craft too when they need to be taken out of the water.

H - The Boat House. Close to the former entrance of the dry dock is a covered arm off the Stroudwater Canal. It was built by the ship canal company in about 1840 to house their ice boat.

This eventually became a facility where work could be carried out on boats under cover. Around the country, many buildings like this have assumed a new role servicing the leisure industry.

I - Wycliffe Boathouse Once home to the RAF, this building now provides accommodation for Wycliffe School and their Boat Club.

Before moving to this site, the school used a boat house on the Stroudwater Canal at Stonehouse. Whilst it was more convenient for the school, the Gloucester to Sharpness Canal provides much more room for modern high-speed rowing boats.

J - The Willow Trust Boats are usually moored close to the Junction. Since 1991 the Willow Trust's volunteers have raised funds to provide trips for people with disabilities.

Each boat is equipped with all the facilities required including lifts for wheelchairs. Large windows have been built in to the boats to ensure that everyone has a good view of the scenery.

K - The Heritage Centre. Initial plans had this building as a sanitary station for the servicing of boats but a large extension was incorporated which now forms an exhibition room. The unit is manned by volunteers from the Cotswold Canals Trust on weekend days. Visitors can learn about the restoration of the Cotswold Canals, buy books, gifts and ice cream and, in summer, take a boat trip, all of which raises funds for the scheme.

L - Sandfield Stables in 1971. Part of this building was built shortly after the ship canal opened to accommodate the horses that towed vessels along the canal.

As steam tugs superseded horse power, the building was used for various purposes including some use by British Waterways until they left site around 2005. As with many other canalside sites, that led to plans for leisure use.

M - Stables Cafe in 2011. During 2008, the old stables building assumed a new role as a cafe. An outdoor two deck timber extension was built on to extend the space available to its customers. The first tenant had good connections with the Junction as his father had just retired as bridge-keeper at the junction itself. More details to be found here: www.thestablescafe.co.uk Phone number 01452 741965.

N - Sandfield Wharf. These sheds were built during the Second World War as a strategic food store. The site was later developed as a wharf for handling coasters bringing imports.

It is worth noting that some of the old wharves in this area have now been developed for private housing . The old oil terminal at Quedgeley was closed down in the 1980s and the surrounding housing developments gained control.

O - Cadbury's Factory opened in April 1916 alongside the Gloucester and Sharpness Canal, south of Sandfield Wharf. The factory produced milk chocolate crumb. Initially, the factory got through 40,000 gallons of milk a year and reached nine million gallons during 1944. In 1964, peak capacity was reached when 75,000 gallons were handled in a single month. Since the company left in 1983 the site has been let to various businesses.

Local Canal Chronology
with thanks to Michael Handford

It may be useful to consider the developments on the local waterways to which Saul Junction is linked, so here is a list of some of the main events over the last 300 years. For in depth histories of the local waterways you would be well advised to seek out the numerous books that are available on the subject.

1730	First Stroudwater Canal Act
1741?-1751?	The Cambridge Canal
1755	The Dallaway Scheme
1759	Second Stroudwater Canal Act
1759-1763?	The Kemmett Canal
1774-1775	Construction of Stroudwater Canal starts
1776	Third Stroudwater Canal Act
1779	Stroudwater Canal opened to Wallbridge in Stroud
1783	Thames & Severn Canal Act
1789	Thames & Severn Canal opened from Stroud to Lechlade
1793	Gloucester & Berkeley Canal Act
1794	Construction of Gloucester & Berkeley Canal begins
1820	Gloucester & Berkeley Canal reaches Saul Junction: Junction Lock constructed on the Stroudwater Canal
1827	Gloucester & Berkeley Canal opened throughout
1845	Great Western Railway opened from Swindon to Gloucester
1927	Thames & Severn Canal closed from Inglesham to Chalford
1933	Thames & Severn Canal closed from Chalford to Stroud
1954	Stroudwater Canal closed
1972	Formation of Stroudwater Canal Society, now the Cotswold Canals Trust
1973	Restoration begins at Bowbridge, Stroud
1978	Restoration work begins on Stroudwater Canal at Eastington
1979	Bicentenary of opening of Stroudwater Canal
1989	Bicentenary of opening of Thames & Severn Canal
2005	Company of Proprietors lease canal to British Waterways since rescinded and leased to Stroud Valleys Canal Co
2006	Major funding approved to restore Stonehouse to Brimscombe
2009	Start of major works to complete restoration of the Stonehouse to Brimscombe section of the Cotswold Canals

Richard Owen Cambridge

Richard Owen Cambridge was the owner of Whitminster House and estate during the latter half of the 18th Century and, as a gentleman of his time, he was very interested in improving the environment of his property. To work at improvements he needed to move heavy loads such as stone from the River Severn and also about his land. Thus, he changed the flow of the River Frome, which crossed his land, so that barges could use the river for the sole purpose of carrying substantial loads around his property.

Nothing exists now of the changes he made to the river, but he was subsequently helpful to the Company of Proprietors when the Stroudwater scheme finally came to fruition by selling parts of his land for canal building.

Company of Proprietors
of the Stroudwater Navigation

Before the canals were built, goods, animals and people used the rivers, local pathways and roads for transport. Then the 1730 Act of Parliament was passed setting out the method by which a canal linking the River Severn to Stroud in Gloucestershire was to be built, managed and operated. The Company of Proprietors of the Stroudwater Navigation was originally formed to carry out the terms of the Act.

The Company still exists, but nowadays is run by a team of voluntary Directors who now ensure that the Stroudwater Navigation is managed for the benefit of the people of Stroud as detailed in the most recent Act of 1954. Currently they are working in partnership with the Cotswold Canals Trust, Gloucestershire County Council and Stroud District Council to ensure the full restoration of the Stroudwater Navigation.

The Company has an archive of documents dating from the 1700s to the present which can be viewed at the Gloucestershire Records Office. The Company has recently formed a group of volunteers who are working towards making the archive more accessible to all. They are seeking Heritage Lottery funding in order to digitise the archive and to put copies onto the Internet so that they can be viewed on line. The picture of a page from one of the Tonnage Books can be seen on the next page. It shows the names of vessels using the canal, the ship's owner, the journey and goods being carried. The various records reflect the history of the times as the quantity of various goods being carried vary with changes in demand and also reflect the competition that arose from the building of the railways.

STROUDWATER NAVIGATION COMPANY.

Account of vessels entering Framilode Lock for Month ending 1890

Date.	Name of Vessel.	Name of Owner.	From.	To.	Species of Goods.	Weight. T.	Weight. C.	Remarks.
August 1	Sisters	Field	Bullo	Stonehouse	Coal	56		
1	Industry	Smart	Chepstow	Stonehouse	Stone	60		
1	Finis	Pearce	Chepstow	Stroud	Stone	64		
1	Try	Pearce	Bullo	Brimscombe	Coal	60		
1	Martha Ann	Smart	Bullo	Brimscombe	Coal	36		
2	Emma	Field	Bullo	Bonds Mill	Coal	56		
2	Perseverance	Smart	Severn	Chalford	Timber	17		
3	Kitty	Pearce	Bullo	Brimscombe	Coal	63		
3	Good Intent	Hicks	Bullo	Lechlade	Coal	29		
3	Sisters	Field	Bullo	Stonehouse	Coal	56		
4	Kate	Wyman	Severn	Bristol	Fruit	3		
4	Elsie	Ayliffe	Bullo	Framilode	Coal	32		
5	Try	Pearce	Bullo	Brimscombe	Coal	60		
6	Economy	Cox	Severn	Bristol	Fruit	2		
6	Industry	Smart	Severn	Chalford	Timber	14		
7	Boat	Ross	Severn	Junction	Empty			
14	Sisters	Field	Bullo	Ebley	Coal	56		
14	Emma	Field	Bullo	Eastington	Coal	56		
14	Seabreeze	Kneel	Bullo	Stroud	Coal	65		
14	Perseverance	Smart	Severn	Chalford	Timber	18		
14	Kitty	Pearce	Bullo	Brimscombe	Coal	63		
14	Economy	Cox	Severn	Bristol	Fruit	2		
15	Rapid	Ward	Bullo	Dudbridge	Coal	58		
15	Betsy	Wood	Bullo	Gloucester	Coal	54		
15	Industry	Smart	Bullo	Bowbridge	Coal	60		
15	Boat	Smyth	Severn	Junction	Empty			
16	Elsie	Ayliffe	Bullo	Frampton	Coal	46		
16	Anne Maria	Wood	Bullo	Gloucester	Coal	70		
16	Kate	Wyman	Severn	Bristol	Fruit	3		

The Junction is Formed

The bend in the Stroudwater arm 100 yards from the Junction marks where the new alignment built by the ship canal company meets the original line of the Stroudwater Canal. Looking back, the original line had no bend at this point and continued through what is now the garden of the Junction House. Old Ordnance Survey maps show a drain running from the canal at this point down the bank and into the River Frome. This presumably had a sluice at the top end beside the towpath which superseded the sluice beside the stop gate as a means of draining the pound for maintenance.

The 1824 map below shows the two alignments with the new one on the right and the old one on the left.

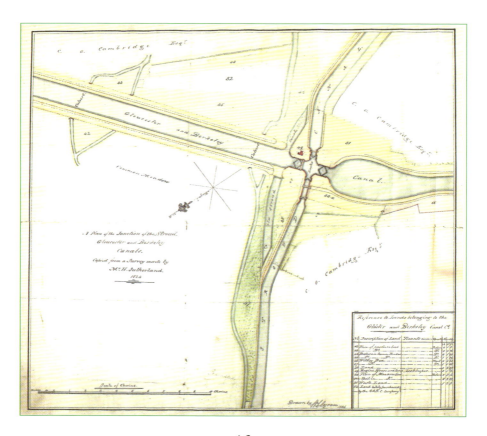

Originally, the Stroudwater (top of photo) had no bend and went straight on along a line at the other side of Junction House. The old line has disappeared under realignments of the watercourses. (Photo: Stroud District Council 2006)

Boats Around Saul

by Lois Francis

Up to the mid 19th century, trows were flat-bottomed, wooden sailing vessels and in the second half of the nineteenth century were mainly ketch rigged. They were open workboats that were able to carry at least 60 tons. They did not have keels, so they were able to negotiate shallow waters. They very often sailed short journeys, but traded as far west as Swansea and Watchet, until the Board of Trade decided that they should only travel as far as Barry and Bridgwater.

The *Reliance* was originally a trow, and carried at least 60 tons to the Stroud Gas works owing to lack of water in the Stroudwater Canal.

Vessels were not allowed to sail on the Gloucester & Sharpness Canal and, although there may be a story to the contrary, it certainly was not a common occurrence.

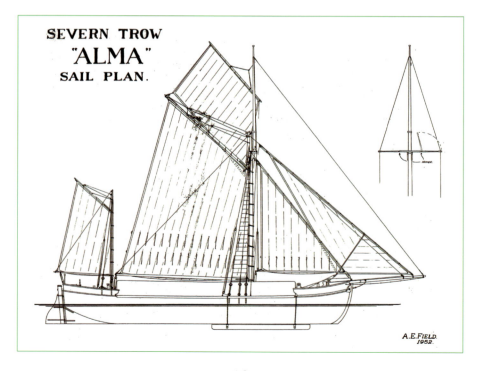

Sailing along the Stroudwater was difficult, and many captains left their sails and masts in the warehouse at Framilode, so that either donkeys or horses could tow them along the canal. Originally, of course, the trows would have been hauled by men!

The crew usually consisted of three or four people and they were responsible for loading and unloading. Their inevitable demise was summed up by a comment made by Captain Jackson, who when asked about the decline of sailing vessels remarked *"I can recollect being thirteen days from Sharpness Point to Cardiff in 'Ely' (a sailing trow) and 3 ¾ hours for the same journey in the Motor Vessel 'Osric'."*

Stroud Barges carried coal from Bullo Dock on the other side of the River Severn, south of Newnham-on-Severn, to Stroud. They were cutter rigged and so only carried one mast, but they were also double–ended and carried about 50 tons of cargo.

A trow being launched sideways at Saul

The Herberts

by Lois Francis with much help from Paul Barnett (Friends of Purton) & Hugh Conway-Jones

Anyone with a surname of Ayland, Camm, Shaw, Hipwood, Rice, Nurse, Butt, Price, Herbert, Aldridge, or Rowles, living near Saul Junction is very likely to be connected to one of the maritime families who built, owned and maintained a variety of boats, bringing cargos from the Midlands, South Wales and Bristol, since the inception of the Stroudwater Canal in 1779.

Saul Junction was a vibrant area for building and maintaining the traditional 'trow' as well as barges. Between 1860 and 1895 twenty-one vessels were built, which included the schooner *Julia* built by Frederick Evans of Saul in 1891. Unfortunately, she was wrecked off Milford Haven in 1906. Other ship–building areas along the Stroudwater included Framilode, Whitminster and Stroud.

The Herberts were one prominent family in the Frampton-on-Severn, Saul and Arlingham area. James Herbert was born in 1850, the son of a farm labourer, but on reaching the start of his working life, he chose to join the crew of the many small sailing vessels that traded along the River Severn and down to South Wales and Bristol. He married Emma Jemima Aldridge in 1869 and they subsequently had 17 children, five of whom became mariners in their own right.

James Herbert progressed to becoming the master of two barges, the *Nelly* and the *Maria*, which each carried 60 tons of coal from the Forest of Dean to wharves along the Stroudwater and the Thames & Severn Canal. In 1876, he became the master of the barge *Reliance* which was owned by the Stroud Gas Light and Coke Co. and for the next twenty years averaged 40 trips a year to Newport, collecting 65 to 70 tons of coal each trip. This brought him and his family enough prosperity for him to relocate from Framilode to Kimberly House at Frampton-on-Severn by Fretherne Bridge.

During the First World War, James sold some of his land at Fretherne Bridge to the Cadbury Brothers, who built a chocolate factory by the Gloucester to Sharpness Canal. The Cadbury brothers developed the site into a busy wharf handling chocolate crumb and also used the extensive dairy industry around them to process chocolate in the factory. As James Herbert's house became the chocolate factory foreman's house, James moved his family to Slimbridge and then to Oatfield, a hamlet between Frampton and Whitminster.

He became owner of the barge *John*, which unfortunately foundered off Lavernake Point carrying silver sand between Barry and Newport. All members of the four man crew were safely rescued and he was able to replace the *John* with a trow called *Victory*.

During this time, James was ensuring that other members of his family were able to become mariners; indeed the vessel *Ada* is one of the 'Purton Hulks', having been abandoned on the banks of the

Captain James Herbert 1850-1930

River Severn at Purton in 1956. She was registered in 1920 to Mrs Flora Herbert, the wife of Joseph, one of James' sons. James eventually decided to supply the Cadbury factory with coal rather than Stroud Gas and Light Company. To enable him to do this, he bought the trow *Industry* in 1919 and fitted the vessel with a motor. The remains of this boat are now buried beneath the car park of the *White Hart* Public House in Broadoak near Newnham-on-Severn.

The fact that James decided to fit a motor to his vessel showed that by the 1920s commercial sailing vessels were facing challenges from motorised boats. By James Herbert's death at the age of 80 in 1930, it was very difficult to keep the sailing fleet profitable in the face of competition from motor barges.

After his death, James Herbert's now quite extensive fleet of small sailing traders was either converted to towing barges or broken up. In his long life he had always championed the sailing traders but his family that followed him as mariners were obliged to change with changing demands.

Sir Lionel Darell 1876-1954

Part of the fabric of Gloucestershire
by Lois Francis with additional material by Tony Ashby

Sir Lionel Darell was described by the Bishop of Gloucester in the 1950s as a *"countryman and a soldier"* and his memoirs were recognised by the Bishop as an important resource for future generations discovering the Britain of the time of recovery from the Second World War. Indeed, in 2011, it is apparent that the personal memoirs of Sir Lionel add great colour to the picture of life on the Severn Vale at the end of the Victorian period of history and stretching into the early and mid-twentieth century.

He was born in 1876, in a large country house in Fretherne (left), which was demolished about 1923 and is now the site of successful plant nurseries. He was educated at Eton, Oxford and then, inevitability, joined the army and was posted to many places over the World. He married and moved to Saul Lodge in 1904, from where he was to become a part of the fabric of life as a magistrate, chairman of many boards of 'Houses of Correction', hospitals and Poor Houses. (Saul Lodge had been built by the Gloucester to Berkeley Canal company for its chief engineer). He was also an avid hunter and fisherman, following hunts and fish all over Britain.

In his memoirs, *Ratcatcher Baronet*, he describes his feelings when he realised Fretherne Court had to go. *"The estate should have to be sold ... It was very sad, but Fretherne Court had no modern requirements, no central heating, and they said we used to burn a ton of coal a day, there... No electricity, the kitchens about a quarter of a mile from the dining rooms, water supply very indifferent, only one or two bathrooms and the drainage system - well"*.

Among his tasks for Gloucestershire, he was very proud to be associated with the Small Holdings Scheme, whereby councils were instructed to set aside holdings of about 40 acres for demobilised soldiers from the Great War to rent and farm. *"However the holdings were too small... I am convinced no man can make a living on a holding of less than 100 acres... many an old soldier of that time 'went under'."*

Sir Lionel Darell seems to have little involvement in the management of any of the Cotswold waterways but was used to fishing in the Severn and, as a County Councillor, was aware of the decisions being made about the waterways. He describes the waterways in the 1920s: *"Severn and Thames Canal Committee - it is all shut up - no water in the canal except at the extreme Severn end."*

He goes on to mourn, or otherwise, the loss of the through canal, *"a canal joining up the River Severn to London Bridge - you could get in, take a ticket at Framilode (where by the way, my grandfather built the church schools, etc - they always thought Framilode was going to be a big port on the river Severn), and row or sail to London, joining the River Severn somewhere up Cirencester way through a long tunnel - well even in those days you would want to know who you were going with?... now derelict, company bust, no water, look at it out of your railway carriage window from Gloucester to Swindon on the left hand side! No, although I live on the banks of the Sharpness and Berkeley Canal (the water will be in my house if they don't soon mend the banks - however, it is nationalised now) canal transportation is too slow, you can go faster in an aeroplane."* We are a little unsure about his geography here, but the sentiment is interesting.

Yet another task involved Sir Lionel as a member of the then Severn Sewers Commission. The Commission was obliged to look after the rheens (big ditches) that flowed into the River Severn. Bailiffs inspected and ordered farmers to clean out any rheen or ditch that had become choked.

As a keen huntsman, he was asked to help in the locating and catching of muskrats that had escaped from a fur farm in Shropshire. The worry was that, as the muskrats liked to build their nests floating in the middle of a stream, they would threaten the banks of the canals in the area, burrowing into the banks and causing leaks. Sir Lionel was amused by the Task and helped a Mr Brocklebank rid the area of the problem.

In 1937 Sir Lionel was surprised by the sight of two submarines, sailing up the canal past Saul Lodge; *"en route for Gloucester where*

they were to tie up for people to go over them - I presume they wanted recruits." An uncomfortable presage to war?

The onset of the Second World War marked a very busy time for the Baronet. This was when his nickname, *The Rat-Catcher Baronet*, was created. As chairman of the County Pests Committee, he had studied the whole country's dire food problem. The country only produced one third of its wants, so two-thirds had to be imported, carried by ships under constant attack from enemy submarines.

The government had estimated that rats destroyed 25 million pounds worth of food each year, because their birth rate from just two rats could expand to 829 further rats in a year. Sir Lionel was instrumental in taking a variety of approaches to preventing rats feeding on waste food and trapping rats that had infested farms, waste tips, school houses, kennels, slaughter houses and, of course, Sharpness Docks, where the rats were known to clamber down the ropes mooring the food ships. Indeed, the enterprise blossomed and involved land-girls, and prisoners of war all housed in caravans and travelling around in order to rid the area of the rat.

Imagine the Baronet's embarrassment when one day, whilst he was away, men from the Ministry of Food arrived at Saul Lodge expecting to inspect the house for food hoarding. They had been told that 2.5 cwt of honey was stored up along with pots of jam, eggs and other provisions. After a very thorough search, the men went away, but the family were never quite satisfied that they had been publicly exonerated.

After the war Sir Lionel Darell continued to be a voice and a presence in the community between the River Severn and the canals. He continued to throw children's parties at Christmas and involve himself in his family. We have here a copy of the recipe Eleanor Ashby, the wife of one of his tenants at Lodge Farm, used to make 69 Christmas Charity puddings, which Sir Lionel gave to various local families. Indeed, a pub on the banks of the river was named the *Darell Arms*. His memoirs do indeed let us into a way of life that has changed and continues to change.

The recipe below for Christmas pudding is found in the recipe book of Eleanor (Nelly) Ashby, grandmother of Jean and Tony Ashby who lived at Lodge Farm, Fretherne at the turn of the twentieth century. It is headed 'Receipt for the Christmas Charity Puddings'. These puddings were made for Sir Lionel Darrell to give to his tenants. Tony believes that each had a pound of beef and a pound of Christmas pudding. Sixty nine puddings were made from the recipe at a cost of £4 19s 1d (£4.95). Milk and eggs are not included in the cost and would have been provided by Lodge Farm.

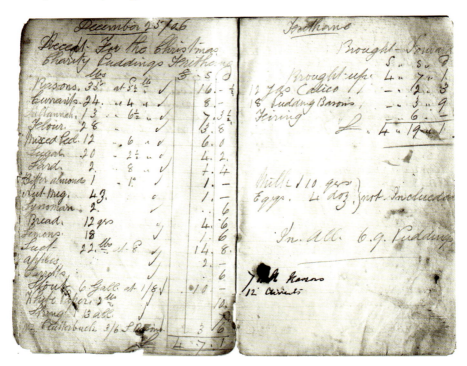

Cadbury's at Frampton
Photos loaned by Ian Parkin

Cadbury's moved to Frampton-on-Severn in 1916 alongside the Gloucester to Sharpness Canal to the south-west of Saul. This selection of photographs is of unknown date but they were probably taken not too long after the factory opened.

A view of the factory looking north-east up the Gloucester to Sharpness Canal in the direction of Saul Junction

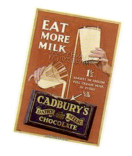

Looking up to the factory from Fretherne Bridge

Looking south-west from the direction of Saul Junction

Cadbury's First Year

An account taken from Bournville Works Magazine June 1917 contributed by Linda Leach

CADBURY'S CONDENSED MILK

It is only a year since the opening of the Frampton factory, in April 1916, but already this offspring of Bournville is emulating its parent, and is growing and developing rapidly.

Summer 1916

By May 1916 the plant was at work, but all of it had not been installed, and the buildings were not finished. During the summer the builders removed their materials, and brought the outside of the factory into order, so that towards the close of the year one could almost imagine that the buildings were mellowing to their surroundings.

All through the summer, the milk arrived daily, and was dealt with speedily. At the same time late instalments of the plant, tardily delivered because of wartime difficulties, came to hand and were put down.

Winter 1916-1917

The winter came, and the milk, after being cleaned and pasteurised, was then taken every day to the railway station for transit to Birmingham and other large towns for sale to the public.

Spring 1917

This year the beginning of April saw the factory again at work on its usual product, but almost at once renewed building activity and alterations to the plant betokened new developments. Canal boats arrived with plant and material, the Frampton staff worked early and late to dispose of it, and by the middle of the month the factory has started on its new line of manufacture - CONDENSED MILK FOR THE GOVERNMENT.

War Work - Bournville Girls

Several Bournville girls, under the charge of Miss Griffin, went down to Frampton and took up their quarters in the village. With an equal number of local girls they started to work - filling, soldering, labelling, case making and packing the new product.

In spite of delays and difficulties due to the necessity for improvisation consequent upon the starting of a new manufacture they adapted themselves to work. Each day the output grew until by the end of the first week substantial progress had been made.

Since then the output has steadily increased, and at the time of writing a large quantity is being produced each week, and despatched to Army canteens in all parts of the country. Needless to say, great interest has been taken in this 'war work' and all concerned have worked, and are working with a will, not only to send the best possible product to the troops, but to ensure that it is worthy to bear the name "CADBURY".

Since the invasion of Frampton by the fair Amazons mentioned above, the girls have been introduced into the proper work, and are shaping well at churn washing and milk handling.

It is interesting to see one gently stirring up the foam milk in a big cauldron like a big heater, a sight, which makes one think of gigantic milk puddings.

Cheese making
In addition to the work in connection with the manufacture of condensed milk, a building has been erected and a plant put down for manufacture of cheese.

Mr George Cadbury's visit
Mr. George Cadbury, who visited the factory in April with Mr. George Cadbury junior, writes: "It was interesting to see how in three weeks new business had been started. It involved a good deal of thought and arrangements - machines for filling the tins, cases for packing them to say nothing of preparing the milk so that it will keep etc. From what we gather the girls are happy and comfortable, though it is quite a new experience for them to be so much out of the world; they had seen no newspaper for some days. Now the firm is arranging for a supply of papers daily to be brought by one of our vans that runs every day to Stonehouse. They have a dining room, as also have the men, with a woman to cook the dinners, etc. Mr Robinson on the afternoon of our visit took the girls to Gloucester to see the Cathedral, etc., he was rather afraid they might be lonely at first in a country place. Lunch was served at Kimberley House, where the foreman Mr J. Wellings lives, in the comfortable room set aside by the firm, and it was interesting to hear the constant rattle of tins coming in full and going out empty - most are delivered by road and not many by water, as at Knighton".

How to Make Chocolate

Roy Preece describes the process used at Cadbury's Frampton factory before its closure

There are three main ingredients used in the process of making the raw chocolate product at this factory - milk, cocoa beans or mass and sugar. At the time these photographs were taken the milk came from local farms in churns which weighed over 50kg when full. The cocoa mass came by boat from Bournville in 100 kilo sacks and the sugar came from Tate and Lyle, also in 100kg sacks so you had to be fit and strong to work at Cadbury's. The boat from Bournville took back the finished chocolate crumb in 50kg sacks. In later years the raw materials came in by road tanker and the finished product was taken to Bournville by the same method.

1 Lorries delivering milk to the factory in churns from local farms

2 Churns inside the factory. Samples for quality were tested in the lab. The man on the left is Bert Wright from Arlingham who played bowls at Cadbury's and was a bell-ringer

3 Milk was stored in large tanks

4 Milk was mixed with sugar (460g per tonne of milk) and heated in these evaporators for two hours

6 The milk/sugar mixture was sucked up from the milk pans into copper kettles and boiled for about 2 hours at 120 degrees

5 Milk was transferred along the horizontal pipe into milk pans

7 Although the milk/sugar mix had been cooked for several hours it still contained crystals of sugar so it was passed through this machine to grind them up. The machine was nicknamed "The Sputnik" as it was installed at the same time as the Russian space programme in the late 1950s - early 1960s

8 The chocolate mass had been milled elsewhere and it was mixed with the milk/sugar mixture in these mixers. The milk came down through a hole in the ceiling. There were 10 of these mixers and the process took about an hour

11 When the trays came out of the oven the chocolate was in a hard solid block. When it had cooled it was tipped out by hand into this crusher and milled up into small pieces before conveyance to the bagging plant

9 The mixture was then poured into these chocolate trays to cool for about an hour and a half

10 The trays were wheeled into ovens, 85 trays per load, and baked for 3 to 4 hours

12 The chocolate was bagged up into 50g sacks and taken to Bournville by canal boat where it was used to make sweets etc. In later years it was stored in large hoppers and taken by bulk road tanker

Memories from the 1920s
of the canal and Frampton-on-Severn
by Commander John W Vick

I was born at Walford House, Frampton-on-Severn in 1917 where my grandfather had lived from 1875. I lived there until 1940. I attended the village school until I was eleven and the headmaster was Harold Nelmes.

My earlier memories of the canal, known locally as the 'cut', were of fishing and swimming there. In the summer, locals went to the 'cows' drink', a shallow access for that purpose and non-swimmers could safely go out as far as the 'ledge' where the bottom dropped steeply. Changing into bathing gear was accomplished in the 'tumps', mounds of clay covered in bushes. They had remained from the time the canal was built and the clay used for lining the bottom.

Left to Right - Grantley Wathan - Eric Lander - Harvey Coleman - Bernard Sims - Bob Cole - Gordon Hobbs - George Taynton - Robin Gleed - Jack Cole - Tony Overbury - Mrs Overbury (standing)

Both adults and children used this as a local lido and many learned to swim there as did I with the aid of a couple of pieces of cork that had floated in from some passing boat.

The banks on either side of the cows' drink offered a good place from which to show off diving skills, providing the dive was far enough out to be over the ledge. One youth called Punch (all the locals had nicknames), whose special feat was to take a running dive from the bank and surface the other side of the canal. Others would swim out to the slow moving timber barges that were towed by steam tugs, climb up to the top of the load and do a high dive into the canal to the applause of the spectators.

All the boys went fishing in the canal. Some proudly carried ancient family rods but many did as I did; obtained a bamboo from a friendly gardener and made a float out of a goose feather. Roach and bream were the main catch apart from the ubiquitous small gudgeon and there were favourite spots from which to fish. One was from a large iron pontoon that had been used to prop up Fretherne Bridge when heavy loads passed and this was moored opposite Saul Lodge.

Frampton always had a connection with the sea and the canal brought this even more into local lives. In the 1920s my neighbour, Mr Herbert, had a one-masted sailing ketch called the *Ada* which he sailed to Ireland from Sharpness and sometimes brought up the canal and moored by the field called the *Cantleas*, the nearest point to his house. Mr Herbert's son Charlie was a contemporary of mine and it was with great delight that I was shown over this boat, which sailed to 'foreign parts'.

In the early 1920s there was no bus service to Gloucester from Frampton but a carrier operated a horse and wagon at intervals for freight and would take passengers. This started from the thatched cottage at the beginning of Whitminster Lane and the doors to the wagon shed are still there.

I was told of the son of a Frampton grocer who went to school in Gloucester by passenger boat. There were two of these, the *Wave* and the *Lapwing*, both steamboats and it was a treat to go to Sharpness on one of these and to have tea at the pleasure gardens.

The nearest railway station was at Stonehouse and Mr Betteridge ran a daily parcel service from the station by horse and cart.

Farming by the Junction

Recollections by Richard Merrett

Richard Merrett farms land adjacent to the Gloucester to Sharpness Canal and the Stroudwater Navigation close to the Junction. In the 1800s his grandfather brought the first cattle to the farm from Newnham-on-Severn via a ferry to Arlingham and then walked them to Whitminster. Other local farmers are known to have banked in Newnham-on-Severn and used the same ferry to cross the River to do their banking.

My grandfather and other local farmers would buy a boat load of coal and have it delivered to the quay in Walk Meadows, just behind the weir.

During the war when we farmed Walk Meadows, the Stroudwater Canal contained mine sweepers. The Germans tried unsuccessfully to destroy the Sharpness Canal by bombing it at Pegthorne Bridge. The first bomb was dropped in the canal. The second hit two elm trees and threw them across the orchard, propping them against two other trees. The third bomb was dropped by the windmill water pump but this bomb did not explode. The fourth bomb was dropped in the canal.

Dairy cow at Packthorn Farm - used by Cadbury's to advertise milk

Filming for a children's television series (*Animal Ark*) was filmed in and around Frampton-on-Severn. Five scenes were filmed at Packthorne Farm.

Cadbury's opened in 1916. Cadbury's collected milk by boat from local bridges and they also collected their own coal by boat at the rate of two boat loads a week. Morelands factory relied on the canal for its supply of timber to make the match sticks. The current Readymix site at Gloucester was originally used as a log pond where a boat loaded with timber and towing two barges of timber plus six tree trunks would deposit the tree trunks in the log pond. Logs would be stacked up where the gas works site at Gloucester is currently located after been retrieved from the log pond.

Shell owned a depot at Quedgeley, where they would deposit oil and petrol that was transported on the canal by their own boats, one of which was called the *Bisley*.

Regent Oil brought their own oils into Gloucester via the canal with their own boats named the *Regent King* which towed the *Regent Jack* and the *Regent Jill* which were oil barges. Another Regent owned boat, the *Regent Queen*, also towed two oil barges. Regent Oil is currently known as Texaco. Esso also had a depot in Gloucester. Esso also had its own boats, the *Wharfdale* and *Foxendale*. All Esso boats had 'Dale' at the end of their name.

MV *Grovedale* © Ken Froud

A Tug Boat Stoker

Recollections by Bob Merrett

My life changed as a result of a conversation with Harry Herbert whose exploits as skipper of the *Severn Industry* cargo ship persuaded me to join the Gloucester Dock Company as a fireman. I was born, brought up and educated in Frampton on Severn. Aged 14 in 1943 I joined the Gloucester Dock Company as a fireman stoker working on the canal tugs.

That first morning I travelled from Frampton to Gloucester by bus to report to the Dock Office to be assigned work and live on tug boat *Speedwell*. My first skipper was quite elderly and 'me being a bit green' he sent me off to a shop at Hempsted to get a tin of elbow grease which was needed as the tug's steam engine was being repaired! There was a crew of three on the tug, the skipper, an engineer and me the stoker. I was to live on board to keep the fire in all the time. The skipper and engineer lived in Gloucester and went home each evening. I had a bunk bed with blankets brought from home. Washing was done in a bucket which also provided the only toilet facilities. Other tugs working the canal were *Staingarth, Iris* and *Mayflower*.

My day began any time from 3 o'clock in the morning as dictated by high tide at Sharpness, as we were expected to arrive at Sharpness an hour before the high tide. I had to stoke up the boiler to get steam pressure up, a job that took about half an hour, before the skipper arrived. Once a week I loaded coal into two bunkers either side of the tug which was enough for the week's journeys.

On arrival at Gloucester, the skipper picked up the day's schedule of work from the foreman in the Company Office; in the event of an early start the schedule would be found pinned to the door. We would circle the dock quays picking up four or five empty barges, and sometimes from other quays like Cadbury's at Frampton. Each barge had a crew of two to steer and operate. We also had a pass man who cycled along the towpath to open up the bridges on the way down the canal. All the bridges opened in the middle, the bridge man opened one side and the pass man the other. The journey down to Sharpness took about four and a half hours. At Sharpness the barges were moored by the bargemen. We would then collect barges loaded with many different goods including timber for Morelands and Nicks, peanuts for Foster Brothers Oil and Cake Mill at Bakers Quay and petrol and coal for Cadbury's. I was paid £1.10s.0d. per week and rarely got home.

After six months I transferred to the *Primrose*, one of three river tugs owned by the Company based at Sharpness. The other two were the *Resolute*, and the diesel powered *Addie*. These tugs had a crew of four; skipper, engineer, mate and stoker. Unlike the *Speedwell* this tug had a kitchen range and I was in charge of cooking. Seamen enjoyed double rations since their work was considered to be important to the war effort. I remember catching an eel in the mud off Portishead, skinning and making a meal out of it.

The tugs worked on a schedule of two weeks in the river and one in the canal. The skippers were very skilled making the hazardous journey down to Avonmouth every day, even in thick fog. There were no radio or radar aids in those days. Having completed a week's canal work, on Sunday evening we would lock down into the tidal basin at Sharpness. We would make four journeys between Sharpness and Avonmouth every day, working every tide, with four hours off in between. Being war time we were aware of the bombing in Bristol but fortunately I was never involved in any incidents. I was paid £2.0s.0d. a week on this tug and remember earning an extra 10s. salvage money when we raced out into the river to help a ship caught in the tide and in danger of crashing into the Severn Railway Bridge.

In 1947 the winter was bad and the tugs went up and down the canal day and night to keep it free from ice. Later that year I was called up and left the Company to join the Royal Artillery. I really loved my time on the tugs; every day was different and I enjoyed the company of the boatmen.

Tug Boat 'Primrose'

RAF Station Saul

Writing in 2003, ex Flight Sergeant Eric Blackman (then aged 81) describes how new air-sea rescue launches and other craft were prepared for service

During the Second World War, my RAF colleague Owen and I had been to Calshot twice and were now Sergeants. Having got a storage unit at Rosneath up and running and considerably expanded we were both posted to Tewkesbury on the River Severn. This was 62 Maintenance Unit (MU) HQ, having left Dumbarton and set itself up in a large boathouse on the Severn. Our old Dumbarton Flight Sergeant was in charge. No sooner had we arrived than we were given a new Marine Tender (MT) and collected two Motor Boat Crews, two fitters and two Aircraft Hand General Duties. We were told to find our way via Gloucester Docks to Saul Junction on the Sharpness Ship Canal. Our kit was loaded on a lorry, which was to meet us there. We were to report to the bridge keeper. We made the voyage without mishap, found the bridge and keeper. He was attended by PC Blick the local bobby. The constable told Owen and me that he would be taking us to our billets and he strongly advised us (as the Sergeants) to choose Mrs Honey at *Springfield* for ourselves. We took his advice and were taken to the little cottage and were welcomed by a rosy-faced countrywoman of about 60. The dining room had a table laid ready with Severn salmon salad, apple pie and cheese. Afterwards, Owen said *"This can't last"*, but it did, the whole time I was there until I was posted to Calshot and Ferry Pool.

Our first task at Saul was to take over the little college boathouse situated at the Junction. Tools, workbenches and heavy equipment fitted into the boathouse while the upstairs rooms turned into an office and crew-room. Our parent unit was at Stoke Orchard and they sent all our requests for equipment to RAF Quedgeley. We had never experienced such prompt attention to our stores requisition forms before. We were told to reclaim a short reach of the Stroudwater Canal and make it ready to receive a number of High Speed Launches (HSL) for storage afloat. There was a swing bridge which had been let down in its cill and not opened for years.

Sledgehammers, axes, mattocks, crowbars, pickaxes and wheelbarrows arrived in quantity from Quedgeley. Soon the canal looked quite navigable. The time was spring 1943. The Air Sea Rescue (ASR) Service was now firmly established in many new bases around our coasts. There was a shortage of HSLs especially as many were being sent overseas. To augment the fleet, builders of GP Pinnaces were given a modified plan which changed the layout. Instead of the after hold and derrick the coamings were raised and formed into a roomy sick bay. A gun turret was added to it and a further turret was fitted in the engine room coach roof. These boats went to bases which could manage with slower craft than the HSLs releasing HSLs for more important and busier bases. HSLs and Pinnaces (ASR) soon started to arrive. Driving mooring posts into the gravel towpath of the canal was a problem soon solved by using screw pickets instead. The Stroudwater proved an ideal, secure, hideaway for the craft, very convenient for replacements to the busy coast bases which were sometimes shot up or mined and convenient for the West Coast ports.

We were soon overwhelmed with work and called urgently for reinforcements. HQ responded by sending seven Under Training (UT) Marine Fitters to help out. HSLs and ASR Pinnaces were arriving every day and none were being sent away and we were getting full with boats. HQ also decided to send some Seaplane Tenders (ST) to Gloucester Docks by road and then floated and towed to Saul by our MT. Two days later there was a phone call to say an ST was already at the docks. Owen and I took the MT, three UT fitters and a bike to the docks. We arrived just in time to join an argument between the lorry driver and the crane driver. The point was how to unload a 41 foot 6 ST weighing seven tons by a steam crane with a safe working load of 5 tons. Owen intervened saying, *"It'll be alright"*, a statement he always made when a risky problem presented itself. The crane was little more than a tin shed on railway lines. It shunted itself amid clouds of steam and smoke on the rails

between the lorry and trailer on which the ST cradle rested, and the basin. Rusty iron callipers and chains secured it to the rails from the crane bogie. With shouts and gestures from Owen, the crane steered its jib up to the maximum elevation and just managed to lift the boat high enough for the lorry to drive clear. With my heart in my mouth I watched the little steaming beast gradually slew its unwieldy load to the water's edge. The callipers visibly lifted the rails with the strain. With the boat safely in the water the crane driver said, *"Don't want no more o' them"*. Little did he know there were about 12 lifts in and out in the pipeline. The following tow went well with one member of the crew cycling ahead to open the bridges for us.

Soon we were likely to run out of mooring space on the canal and eyes turned to the pound above the grounded swing bridge. Taking advantage of the mechanical bent of some of our UT Fitters Marine we set them to work freeing the bridge and getting it into the swing again. The bridge opened easily to cheering onlookers and the consternation of the local bread van driver who suddenly appeared round a nearby bend in the lane. Hitherto much of our labours were viewed with indulgent amusement by the locals, especially all those who worked on the cut. The swing bridge episode marked a change of view and all concerned appeared more co-operative.

We had already enjoyed a good deal of hospitality from the scattered residents of Saul. We had invitations to tea, supper and drinks from far flung outposts like Frampton, Framilode and Arlingham. Jolly summer tennis parties with the family of the Vicar of a nearby parish, I remember with pleasure. To help pay for the War villages and towns all over Britain held a 'Wings for Victory Week'. Saul, of course, had to be in the swim especially as they had their very own RAF Unit. We were asked to spearhead that year's effort to raise funds.

Mrs Honey did not approve of the methods by which money was raised. The system was that well-heeled people in the district (and there were a few) were canvassed to give more or less valuable small personal items to be auctioned for the fund. Successful bidders were required to buy National Savings Bonds to the value of the item 'bought'. Mrs Honey complained that this resulted in many valuables being 'sold' for a fraction of their true worth and nameless people taking an unfair advantage. Mrs Honey knew that I had just celebrated my 21st birthday. She also knew that my relatives had taken advantage of wartime shortages and sent me cheques instead of goods, as presents. In other words she knew I was in funds. She suggested that I should go to the auction for Wings for Victory especially to run the prices up. She went along as well to do the same thing while I underwrote her if she overstepped the mark. On the night everything went according to plan. It took some time before the competitors realised that a mere RAF Sergeant was a genuine bidder. One 'mistake' I made was being landed with a gigantic and beautiful soup tureen with lid and ladle by Spode with about a gallon capacity. I presented it to Mrs Honey who served us with many a rabbit stew or tripe and onions supper.

While all this was going on in deep Gloucestershire the war was being waged around our coasts. The concept of Air Sea Rescue had changed from the original idea that fast launches would be called from harbour to rescue ditched airmen at sea. A better idea was to send the boat to sea ready for any casualties that may have been in trouble. East Coast bases sent their boats out at 5 am to rendezvous positions, every 20 minutes. Recall was usually some time before midnight. A more comfortable boat for these duties was devised by the British Power Boat Co. Southampton. They were not quite as fast as the original HSLs but life on board all day, especially in rough weather, was more tolerable. The new boats were known as Hants and Dorsets after the double deck based as they had a high deck-house giving them a double deck appearance. ASR Pinnaces and Hants and Dorsets made the bulk of the craft moored in our cut. Enemy action led to abandonment of bright yellow decks which was supposed to signify the non-combatant and one gun turret was being replaced by an Oerlikon canon on the stern to ward off hostile aircraft.

One evening Mrs Honey's telephone rang with a message for me. HQ Tewkesbury informed me that a dispatch rider was bringing orders to our office at the Junction and I was to meet him. I jumped on my bike and duly received a brown paper envelope marked 'MOST Secret'. RAF Saul had grown in size. Armourers, electricians, wireless mechanics and other specialist trades had been added to our ranks. Newly arrived vessels could be put into operational mode by our own staff.

Opening the orders I was appalled by their content. We were required to 'make operational and ready for service' no less than four Hants and Dorset HSLs, with rations for four crews for two days, full ammunition and fuel, ready for the crews to arrive the following night and ready to sail within 48 hours. Two of the boat numbers listed were above the swing bridge. I began to feel that Owen's oft repeated remark, *"It'll be alright"*, had got through to HQ somehow. Fuel and water we could probably manage, but food? On my way back to *Springfield* that lovely summer's evening I stopped off at the village shop and knocked up the two old girls who ran it. Rations for two days for 36 men? Without payment? Without coupons? *"That will be alright, if you say so, Sergeant"*. Bless them. They chose the items including tomato sauce and salt and pepper and made up eight cartons, two for each boat, which were picked up by a truck from RAF Stoke Orchard.

Meanwhile we towed the boats down to the chocolate factory where there was a quay and fresh water. The stores were loaded on board there, including ammunition, also from Stoke. The launches all had to be towed by our one Marine Tender. These triple screw 1500 hp boats did not handle well in confined waters. Drag on the gearboxes produced a speed of six knots in neutral when new.

Some of our airmen were living out with their wives and there were plenty of girl friends too. We asked for volunteers to man the galleys of the boats and cook a meal ready for the crews arriving after a long rail journey. This scheme proved a great success and a good time was had by all.

Next morning road fuel tankers arrived to fill the launches. Frightful snag – they had no pumps being used to supply by gravity to underground tanks. Someone had the brilliant idea of mooring each launch beneath Frampton Bridge and driving the tanker to the middle of the bridge so giving the height required for the transfer. The four boats sailed for Sharpness on time.

Shortly after this episode I was posted to Calshot at my own request and found myself coxswain of Ferry Crew No 8. I did two or three trips to Saul and Dunbarton now completely unrecognisable as 230 MU. My exploits following this account are to be found in my book *Airman at the Helm*, published by Peter Mason but sadly now out of print.

Boatyard & Drydock

The south east corner of Saul Junction was for many years shared by private boatbuilders and the ship canal company's maintenance craftsmen. The former built and repaired small sailing vessels, and the latter constructed and maintained bridges, lock gates and maintenance craft.

When the dry dock was built by the ship canal company in 1869, it originally had gates at each end to provide a link between the two canals across one corner of the Junction, and these were made wide enough for the ship canal company's steam dredger which was too wide to use the normal route. This was important because the ship canal company was obliged to keep the Whitminster pound of the Stroudwater free of mud as a condition of receiving River Frome water that way, and it was more efficient to get their steam dredger to do the work than to rely on an old hand-operated spoon dredger. The opening at the Stroudwater end of the dock has subsequently been shut off by a wall, but its position can still be seen.

The boatyard today is owned by RW Davis & Son Ltd who operate a thriving business from the site. The crane is a Potain fixed tower crane with a radius of 120 feet and a capacity of 10 tonnes. It is used for day to day boatbuilding operations as well as the craning of cruisers and small narrowboats.

Jones's Junction

Writing in 2011, Tony Jones recalls 'his' Junction

I probably started going down to the Junction when I was 11 or 12 taking my fishing rod tied to the crossbar of my bike. Coming down the lane to Walk Bridge, the first indication of the presence of the Sharpness Canal would often be a ship's siren blowing for the bridges and I would race down to the bridge and along the Stroudwater towpath so not to miss the vessel's passage. The thrill would be seeing a coaster towering over the trees, or a plume of smoke (and the shrill of a steam whistle) would indicate that *Speedwell* or *Mayflower* was on the way with a train of barges. I would arrive breathless to gaze spellbound as a ship eased through the bridge'ole with inches to spare, or admire the nonchalant steerers leaning on the tillers of a succession of deep laden barges behind the bustling tug.

The bridgeman then was Mr Spiers, a former *Severn and Canal* boatman. In those days the bridgeman's jobs and the houses went to the older bargemen or boatmen who brought a lifetime's experience and commitment to the job. Mr Spiers was a taciturn old gentleman, but he unbent to my frequent presence and diffident questions, and I gained an inkling of the hidden world of the canals and 'longboats' up the river.

I did some fishing, but never had the patience of a dedicated angler and such a sedentary occupation soon lost its charm when there was so much to see and explore round the Junction. The few pleasure boats in the Stroudwater arm then were mostly elderly motor cruisers or houseboats and only a couple were converted narrowboats. Above Walk Bridge some big pre-war motor yachts, two of which appeared to have been originally steam powered, were lying in a derelict condition but they were soon towed away and I don't know what happened to them.

I only remember two pleasure boats by name - the converted narrowboat *Sarah*, a seven-planker (very deep hulled) former horseboat - and the *Hilo*, a graceful and beautifully kept 1930s yawl which laid up by the Stroudwater footbridge through the winter months. The owner of the *Hilo*, a retired Naval Officer and his wife were friendly, and on inclement days I would be invited aboard for tea and biscuits, thrilled to be in a real boat's cabin to gaze spellbound at their charts as they told me of their voyaging. One summer, they went as far as the Mediterranean coast of Spain.

Davis's yard in those days was kept busy mainly repairing commercial craft. Quite a few trows then still survived working as towed or motorised barges, and it was fascinating seeing them on the dock being repaired. Some of the older shipwrights and the retired trowmen and seafarers who, on fine days, would come to watch work going forward could remember some vessels under repair being built! The seemingly effortless craftsmanship in working large oak timbers was fascinating to watch. Virtually 'by eye' they shaped replacement oak planks, up to two inches thick, steamed them until relatively pliant and then wedged, hammered and spiked them into place. Some of the trows were really ancient vessels, but had been built to massive strength, I was told that even if half their frames had rotted away they were still sound enough to carry cargo. A telling remark by one of the old hands, when queried as to whether one of the more decrepit craft was worth repairing, was *"as long as we can find enough solid wood to drive the spikes into we'll have a go"*!

Boarding trows laid by at the Junction, I was struck by the comfortless accommodation their hardy crews took for granted in the past. The crew's quarters in the foc'sle consisted of claustrophobic coffin-like bunks in which one couldn't stretch out - our forbears were, reputedly, of shorter stature! Furnishings consisted of bench lockers and a triangular table. Heating was a cast iron 'bottle stove', the only light from a couple of grimy bullseyes in the deck, sanitary facilities a bucket. The deckhead was very low, the smaller trows barely boasting sitting headroom. The only ventilation came through the entrance hatch and the atmosphere, a compound of damp/rot/mould/coalsmoke/old rope/paint/tar and mud in the chain locker, must have been an unwholesome fug when battened down in bad weather. Apart from the fact that the Master's cabin aft accommodated him in solitary dignity, the only mitigation of its Spartan comfort was a little more illumination from a small opening skylight, and heating by tiny built-in fireplace. I asked Mr Spiers how they cooked and ate and he said it was just *"kettle, frying pan and poaching"* and his Father remembered when they cooked on an open fire in a sandbox hearth on deck. Many years later I saw such open cooking hearths still in use on West Indian schooners, but in such a balmy climate it would be no hardship. In winter snow and rain on the trows it would be cold comfort and cold grub!

As a teenage Sea Cadet I enjoyed camping and boating at the Junction. We had a very decrepit wooden hut built during the War from packing cases which had contained parts and equipment for the high speed RAF launches assembled there and tested on the canal. We slept on 'donkey's breakfasts' (straw-filled sack mattresses) and cooked on a coal range with coal begged or stolen from Davis's boiler house. Our domestic water we fetched in the jollyboat in a couple of milk churns from a tap at Sandfield Wharf. For ablutions we used the canal. Our fleet of boats consisted of a massive ex-navy launch with a six-cylinder petrol engine but to go for a run with it we had to all 'chip in' for the fuel! It was kept in the boathouse behind the shipyard. Next was the 16ft jollyboat which could be both sailed and rowed, and there were several ex-commando canoes (still with the fittings to stow 'limpet' mines and sten-guns!).

In those far-off pre Health & Safety days, apart from the ceremonial events of the day such as 'Colours' and ' Sunset' musters, and mealtimes, we were generally under the (mostly ineffectual) supervision of a Cadet Petty Officer. The adult Officers and NCOs left us much to our own devices and adjourned to the conveniently adjacent *Drum and Monkey*! We boated, swam and skylarked around the Junction and up and down the main canal, and canoed on the Frome, or up the Stroudwater as far as the Bristol Road. We did have some lifejackets, bulky 'Board of Trade' pattern, but there was no compulsion to wear them unless you were a non-swimmer. By modern standards our adult supervisors would be considered grossly negligent, but our activities were always under the eyes of the local working canal community, and no transgression went unnoticed or unreported. Though our elders could well be sojourning in the pub, our transgressions were

Tony Jones (right) with brother Trevor stands proudly on his pontoon conversion shortly after launch by crane at the Junction

sure to come to their attention and suitable punishment such as 'spud duty' or 'waterboat crew' followed!

More recent acquaintance with the Junction came after I left the Navy in 1965 when I decided that a little canal boating would be enjoyable. To become a boatowner with minimal expenditure was a simple enough matter then. A former 20ft. army bridging pontoon was purchased, converted to a handy little outboard cruiser at Stroud Sea Cadet Headquarters, (where I had now, in my maturer years, become a Chief Petty Officer instructor) to accommodate our family. On completion she was roaded down to the Junction and 'launched' by the hand-operated crane at Davis's. Naturally, we kept her moored in the Stroudwater Arm when not cruising. During holidays we covered a fair extent of the Midland waterways. After we sold her in 1968 she continued a well travelled life, and has now ended her active life as the only known surviving 'pontoon conversion' preserved ashore at the Ellesmere Port Boat Museum.

After that, the family went into working boating. During our latter years in the retail coal trade our pair *Comet* and *Betelgeuse* brought coal down the Severn and along the Sharpness Canal through the Junction.

'Comet' in the drydock in the mid 1970s

Saul Marina

The latest addition to the Saul Junction scene is the Marina. Work started in 2007 to excavate the mooring basins from the field to the south-east of the Junction. The land here was at a slightly lower level than the canal which runs on an embankment. Officially opened on 25th April 2008, it took seven months to complete. Around 50,000 tonnes of mud was moved (though none left site), 12 million gallons of water were pumped in and 6km of jetty was laid. Provision was made for 284 boats.

Construction was undertaken by *Land & Water* who ran the facility at first before selling to *Lakeland Leisure Estates*. The Marina is entered from the Stroudwater Canal. Perhaps this makes it the biggest marina on the shortest canal, at least until restoration progresses beyond Walk Bridge!

Below: Saul Marina in August 2011

Top: The marina during construction in January 2008
Above: Nearly there in 2008 and cutting the tape at the opening ceremony

www.junctionheritage.org.uk
working with www.cotswoldcanalsknowledge.org.uk

The project came into existence in 2003, when British Waterways and the Cotswold Canals Trust invited local residents in the vicinity of the Heritage Centre, Saul Junction, Gloucestershire, to form a heritage group focused on the parishes that are linked by the waterways that meet at Saul Junction. The decision was taken to form an electronic archive of memories, memorabilia and photographs and to make this available to all via the Internet. We are grateful to the Heritage Lottery Fund which granted funding with which we bought the necessary hardware and software and web hosting and other equipment to enable us to set up the website. Members of the Junction Heritage team work with the Cotswold Canals Knowledge group on the development and promotion of educational materials, using the archive and other sources. This book is a new venture for the group.

Restoration of the Cotswold Canals took a leap forward in July 2001 with the formation of the Cotswold Canals Partnership. The aim of the partnership is to build on work achieved to date and deliver the full restoration of the Cotswold Canals. The members of the partnership are: Stroud District Council, Cotswold Canals Trust, The Waterways Trust, South West Regional Development Agency, Gloucestershire County Council, Wiltshire County Council, Gloucestershire First, Gloucestershire Rural Community Council, Environment Agency, Gloucestershire Soc for Industrial Archaeology, Learning & Skills Council, Cotswold Water Park Society, Inland Waterways Association, South West Tourism, Co. of Proprietors of the Stroudwater Navigation, North Wiltshire District Council, Cotswold District Council.

With origins dating back to 1972, the Cotswold Canals Trust is the thriving group of over 6000 members who support restoration of the Stroudwater and Thames & Severn Canals. Regular monthly social gatherings and a quarterly magazine - *The Trow* - enable members to keep updated on the progress of restoration and to enjoy the canals whilst many support the cause by way of physical help. Some like to crew a trip boat, others man the publicity unit around the country. Of course many members enjoy restoring and maintaining the canal itself. More from: www.cotswoldcanals.com   Phone 01453 752568   mail@cotswoldcanals.com